Bollywood Diary *Goher Iqbal Punn*

Table of Contents

Chapters	Page No.
Foreword by Sshard Malhotra	02
Foreword by Donal Bisht	03
Foreword by Maushmi Udeshi	04
Preface by Goher Iqbal Punn	05
Kishore Kumar - Legend and Versatile Genius of Hindi Films	07
Beware of Kishore Kumar – The Eccentric Behavior of the Legendary Singer	12
Gulzar – the Man Whose Creativity Knows No Limits	15
The Hidden Love Story of Reena Roy and Mohsin Khan – Jaya Bachchan's Role in Helping Her Decide for the Pakistani Cricketer	18
Salman Khan Slapped Katrina Kaif in Public, Pushed Aishwarya Rai and Smashed a Bottle on Somy Ali's Head	21
Anu Malik Drove into a Dark Empty Place and Unzipped His Pants and Asked Me to: Bollywood Singer	23
You Need to Give Sexual Favors If You Want to Get Big Break in Bollywood	26
When a Famous Bollywood Film Director Had to Sleep with a Widely Popular Film Producer to Get His Bollywood Break	29
Are Journalists the Representatives of the Celebrities?	31
Does Pakistan Need Bollywood?	33
Do We Have Courage to Say 'Yes' to Item Numbers?	36
Bollywood Awaits Donal Bisht – Is She Ready?	39
From Modeling to Acting and Now Film Censor Board – Maushmi Udeshi	41

Foreword

Bollywood Diary consists of the columns written by Goher Iqbal Punn, who is an experienced showbiz journalist, and it is his first book on Bollywood. The writer has expertise on the topic and is laced with good writing skills which are impressive and attention-grabbing. The book also got me nostalgic as it contains a number of stories on yesteryear's celebrities.

The book is sure to impress the readers particularly the Bollywood buffs, as it carries very attractive content on celebrities (from past to present) and Bollywood fraternity. Punn's massive knowledge on cinema industry is quite vivid from his writings. He has brought many hidden facts to light, which are not only shocking but also informative for the readers. Goher stuck to truth while revealing the facts about celebrities and entertainment industry. He did not spice up the content as normally happens in tabloid journalism rather he unzipped the details as and when they happened. Thus, the readers will be destined to get true facts.

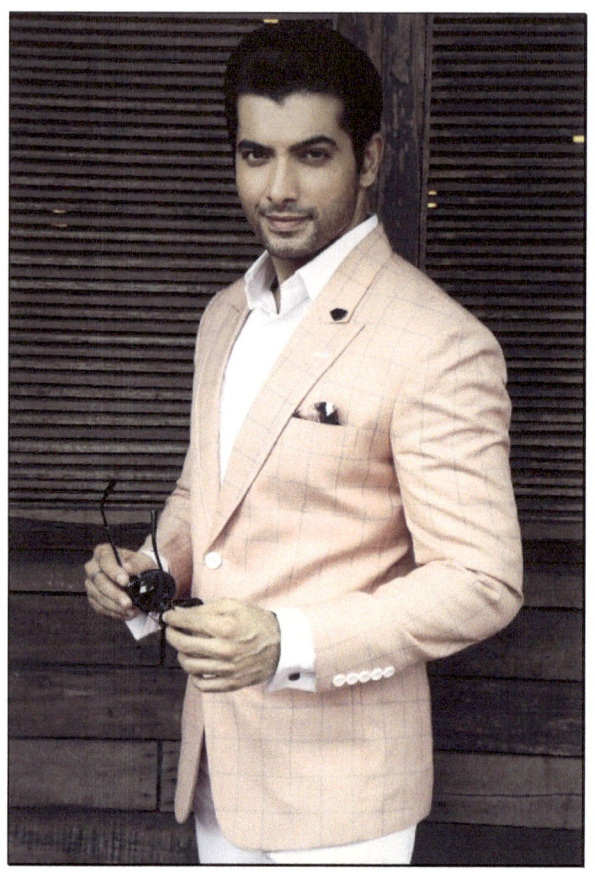

Sshard Malhotra

This experienced journalist's repertoire includes many big names of media industry such as BBC (London), Screen (a weekly entertainment magazine by the Indian Express), Bollywood Hungama (Mumbai) and many others across the world. Media giants like Newsweek (USA), Christian Science Monitor (USA) and The Times (London) have taken Goher's expert opinion on Bollywood and Indian celebrities.

'Bollywood Diary' is a result of his outstanding effort and will steal the hearts of movie lovers. It is recommended to be read and put into your library's shelf. For researchers, it will be like an encyclopedia. I wish him all the best for this book and all of his future endeavors.

Sshard Malhotra

(Indian Television and Film Actor)

****

Foreword

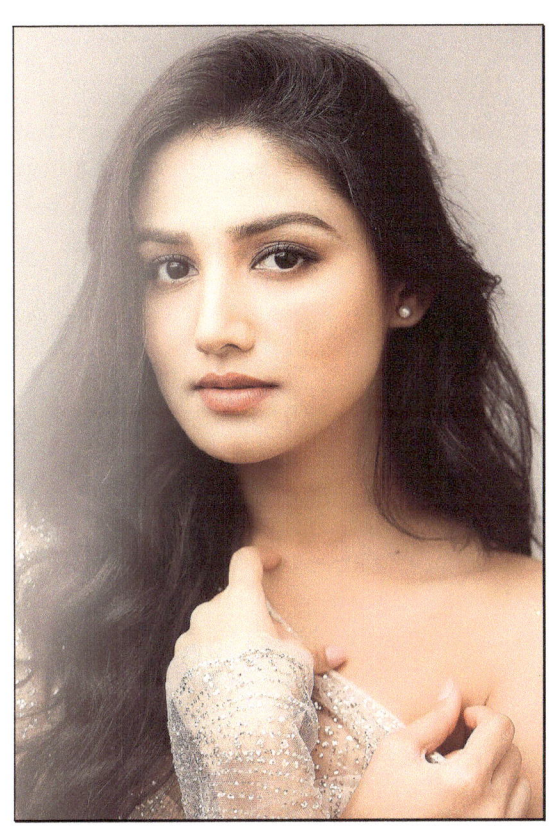

Donal Bisht

It has been one and half year since I know Goher Iqbal Punn. And I must say that it has been a great association so far. I know him as a journalist. His brilliance is that before calling, he completely studies the history of the person and then puts up the questions. This makes the interviewee (celebrity) become quite comfortable. I have seen that he is not into controversial write-ups. In his writings, the reader gets to know how positively he portrays the things and exactly writes what is told. Goher does not mold the things for masala, so I trust him for his writings.

And now that he has written a book I am sure it is not fabricated. It would reveal the real truth and the readers would definitely enjoy reading it. Since this book is the sum up of his vision, his journey over the years and it is just not some years rather it is over a decade or so, thus it would be quiet interesting from all aspects. And *'yes'*, he has been always a great human, humble and sweet in talking. I wish him congratulations and good luck for his first book.

Donal Bisht

(Indian TV Actress)

****

Foreword

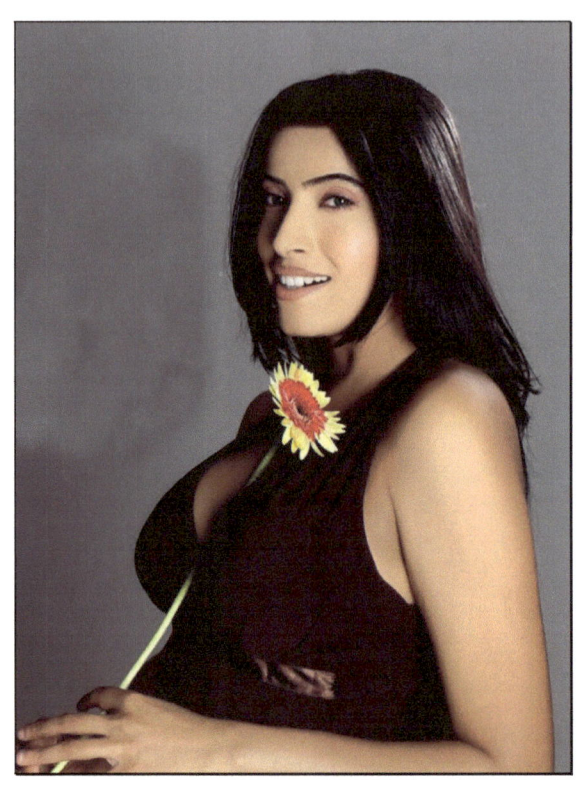

Goher Iqbal Punn is a very experienced Journalist and I know him since almost the beginning of my career say around 15 years. He has always kept in touch and always written great things about me and my work in the media for which i am extremely grateful to him for believing in my talent and for his kind support. He writes extremely well and is not afraid to say the facts. He reveals as they happen and without any pretense which I like the most about him. Goher is an extremely sweet and sensitive human being who is passionate about his work and I am lucky to have known him for so many years. I am sure his book will give the real insights to the bitter facts of our Industry and will be a great eye opener for the masses especially the ones who are unaware of the nasty and horrible facts of our so called most beautiful looking film and advertising industry. I wish him all the very best for this new endeavor of his career and I am sure as always he will be noticed and recognized with flying colours as a great writer of today's time. God Bless him!

Maushmi Udeshi

Maushmi Udeshi

(Model, Actress and Member Advisory Board of Film Censor Board, India)

****

Preface

'Bollywood Diary' is my first book. The excitement factor is quite high and I hope my readers will appreciate my efforts consumed on writing this book. It consists of my columns published under the titles *'Grapevine'* and *'Spilling the Beans'* on various online publications. Out of these, one column written on the legendary late music genius Kishore Kumar *'Legend and Versatile Genius'*, was published in Screen (a then weekly magazine for movies by Indian Express, which also conducts Star Screen Awards in association with Star Plus channel). Apart from the published ones, I have written few columns solely for this book. *'Bollywood Diary'* is actually peekaboo and takes out the hidden stories from the lives of celebrities. It contains many eye-opening truths, scandals and everything about Bollywood stars. I tried to be unbiased while unzipping the facts – some of you will like my efforts while others can hate me. I do not want to be juicy and like to spice up the stories rather would like to bring the truths out which happen off-screen and behind the curtain.

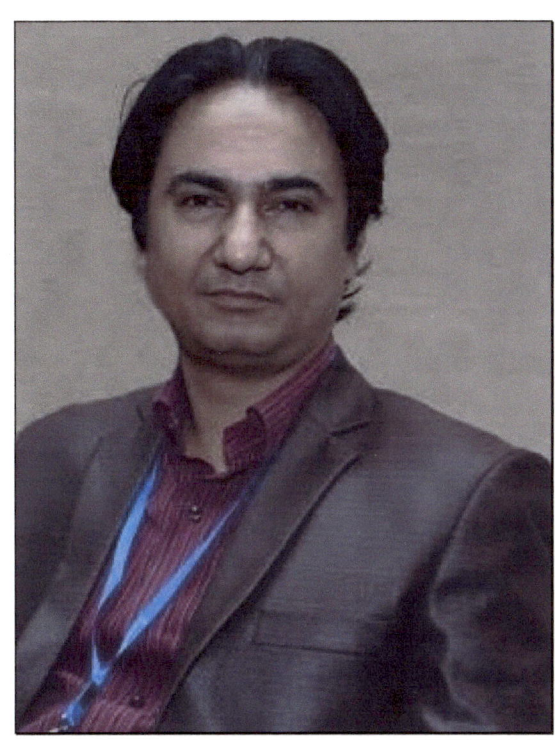

Goher Iqbal Punn

A journalist's prime duty is to get the facts out and this is what I do and have been doing since the beginning of my career. I am to justify my job and the same I have dolled up in this book. All age groups have been taken into consideration during the writing process, thus you will find content engraved on yesteryear to present celebrities.

I have been in the field of journalism since my college days i.e. since year 1994, but my association with Bollywood journalism started in 2002. In my long career, I have worked with *BBC (London), Screen (Mumbai), Bollywood Hungama (Mumbai), Planet Bollywood (New York), Glamsham (Mumbai), One India (Bengaluru), India Info (Kolkata), Bollywood City (Toronto), Bolly Spice (Toronto), Way to Bollywood (Kuwait), Radio Sargam (Leeds), Clickwala (London), Daily Times (Lahore), The Post (Lahore), The Business (Lahore)* and to name a few.

I am an entrainment aficionado and since my childhood I have been a big Bollywood enthusiast. The world of showbiz is magical. And since I have been associated with the glittering abode of cinema, it is in my blood now. Once you have become a part of it, you cannot live without it. It's a magical world.

Media moguls such as *The Christian Science Monitor (USA)*, *Newsweek Magazine (USA)* and *The Times (UK)* apart from others have taken my opinion on Hindi film industry and its celebrities. Research students often approach me for my views and one of them was from a Spanish university *'The National Distance Education University (UNED)'*.

In the end, I would like to thank Sshard Malhotra, Donal Bisht and Maushmi Udeshi who wrote forewords for my book. These three are absolute gems of the entertainment industry of India. I admire their talents, so do the masses. My rapport with Maushmi and Donal in particular is very sweet and they both are very nice, amiable and great human beings.

Goher Iqbal Punn

(Bollywood Analyst, Film Critic, Music Reviewer & Columnist)

****

1

Kishore Kumar - Legend and Versatile Genius of Hindi Films

What would you call a man who's good at singing and dancing, acting and mimicking, writing and composing, making you laugh and cry, all at the same time? Kishore Kumar of course. He was one of a kind in Hindi films, a multi-faceted personality, a man who was in love with music. A man who was sensitive but who also loved playing pranks. These opposing qualities led people to label him a complicated personality and till the end Kishore remained an enigma to Bollywood, to his family, friends and fans. He worshipped music, and the words of Rabindranath Tagore held true for him. The world speaks to me in pictures my soul answers in music.

Kishore was born on August 4, 1929, to a middle class family in Khandwa. His father Kunjhalal Ganguly was a lawyer by profession, while his mother Gauri Devi was an educated woman from a wealthy family. Named Abhas Kumar Ganguly, Kishore was the youngest of four children Ashok Kumar was 20 years older than him, and Kishore's only sister Sati Devi was 15 years older to him Anoop Kumar, Kishore's second brother, was five years older to him.

In his early years, the singer was a very naughty boy. He never seemed tired of seeking amusements, and Anoop and Sati were his partners in pranks. He was very close to his sister who was always supportive of his sense of humor. The interaction between Kishore and Ashok was minimal since the elder brother left home to study law after securing a degree in science. The two brothers met occasionally, when Ashok would visit the family.

His parents sent Kishore in a renowned school at Khandwa, but he was never interested in education, and hated reading books and the discipline in school that seemed to curb his natural steam. Since a child, he was always inclined towards music. He used to sing for his family members, and would be presented with token money. He was often asked to sing Ashok Kumar's song *'Main Bban Ki Chidiya'* from the film *'Achyut Kanya'* since he was good at imitating.

Later Kishoreda (people used to call him da with respect) started singing K L Saigal's songs. Meeting Saigal was his only wish which, unfortunately, never came true since Saigal passed away soon after Kishore's entry in the Hindi film world.

Way back in his childhood days, Kishore had told brother Ashok that he wanted to sing for the films. But the elder brother wasn't encouraging and said his voice was not good enough for singing. This upset Kishore for days, but he worked on his voice and made his mark in the Hindi film industry, and elder brother Ashok had to admit to his natural talent.

When Kishoreda entered Hindi films, Ashok (who by then had established himself as an actor) thought it was best for Kishore to pick up acting by doing small roles in films. Though Kishore did act, his heart was into music. He was pretty confident he would make it as a singer, initially he was rejected many a times with the reason *"Your voice is no good"*.

While shooting for *'Ziddi'*, music director Khemchand Prakash heard Kishore sing and was impressed with his style. Parkash went straight to Ashok Kumar and told him. *"This boy has a future as a singer and he will rule the singing world one-day"*.

Parkash even offered Kishore a song to sing, which he rendered in typical Saigal style *'Marne Ki Duayen Kyon Maangoon'*. Kishore impressed S.D Burman too, who heard him bathroom singing while he was visiting Ashok Kumar. When Kishore came out of the bath S D Burman complimented his singing and told Kishore that he must develop a style of his own. It was S D Burman who made Kishore a famous singer when he took him to sing *'Mere Sapno Ki Rani'* for the movie *'Aradhana'*.

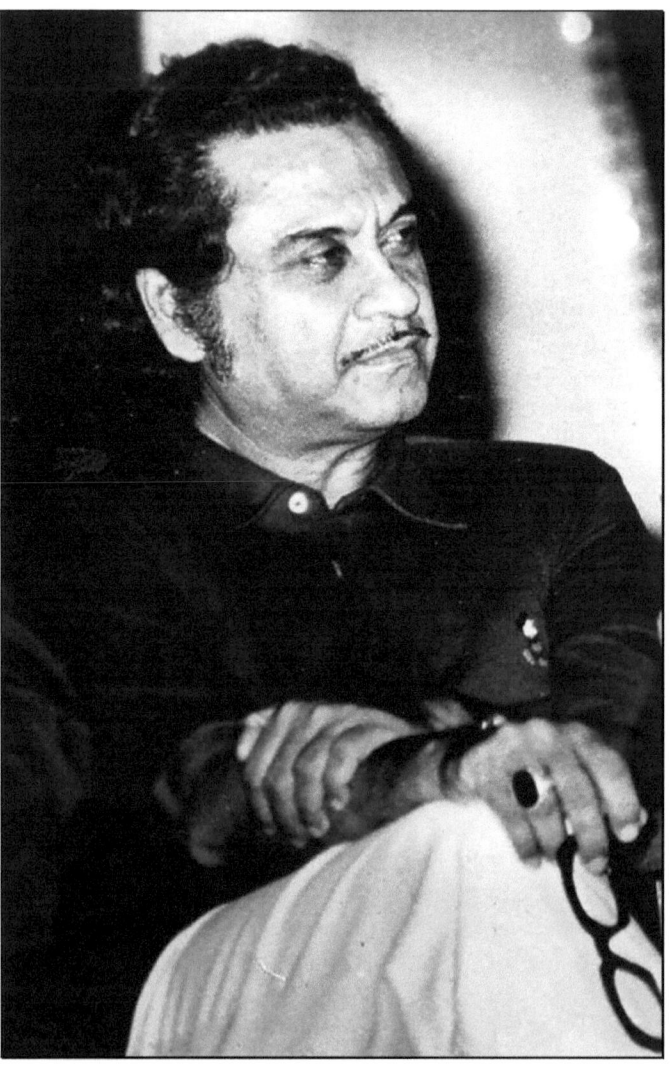

Kishore Kumar

There was no one with a musical background in Kishore's family except his maternal uncle Dhananjay Banerjee, who was a classical singer. But Kishore never even trained under him. It was Ashok who learnt music from the well-known classical singer Saraswati Devi. Kishore, on the other hand, bought Saigal's records which served as his guru.

Kishore would recall how elder brother Ashok called him and Anoop a pair of donkeys. *"I could do little else besides sing"*, he had said.

With a passion for music Kishore always ended up composing different tunes for different subjects. For example, he once composed a tune for a paragraph on the theory of population.

If Kishore' singing left its mark, his performances too were unforgettable. He will always be remembered in the film *'Padosan'*. In which he mimicked his maternal uncle – long hair, kajal in the eyes, constant betel-leaf chewing and the works Kishore proved his acting prowess in tragic and comic roles in the films. He produced and directed most of his films, besides writing, composing and singing for them.

One of Kishore's ambitious films was *'Jhumroo'* which he produced, directed, acted and composed music for. The film did well at the box office. He then made an uncharacteristically serious film *'Door Gagan Ki Chhaon Mein'*, based on the relationship between a father and his mute son. It was released in 1964. This film revolved around the concept of war too. The singer's son Amit Kumar played the character of his son in the film. This film went on to win many national and international awards.

The music of the film was soft and simple, something which people could listen to in isolation. It is an interesting thing to note that when *'Door Gagan Ki Chhaon Mein'* was released, there were only 10 people in theatre too see it. Kishore was very upset as he had put all his energies in the making of his film and interestingly, he himself was in the hall among the audience of 10 people. But within a few days, the halls began to fill up and the film broke all previous records. The success the film made Kishore happy and more enthusiastic about making more films on sensitive subjects, as he himself was a very sensitive person in life. But he never revealed his sensitive side to the world. Kishore then went on making more films like *'Door Ki Rahi'*, *'Badhti Ka Naam Daadhi'*, *'Zindagi'* and *'Door Wadion Mein'*.

The singer was a restless soul which led him doing many things all at the same time. Once a stage show with him and Lata Mngeshkar was arranged in Landon, Kishore was actually surprised that Lata ji had agreed to do a show with him, but at the same time was much worried about her discipline. She was known to never step on stage without proper rehearsal, while on the other hand, Kishore liked to take things easy. A problem arose when they both had to go on stage. No one could decide who should go first. Kishore insisted that Lata ji go first, as she was his senior. But Lata refused to sing first, and instead went on stage and introduced Kishore and praised him a lot, but also mentioned that she called him on stage first because he was older to her. Kishore replied with a laugh, *"Yes, I am one month and 24 days older than her"*. It had the audience in splits. Kishore was famous for his eccentric behavior with his colleagues and heroines.

If the world was his fan, Kishore was a crazy fan of Topol. Once he was in London and was scanning the newspaper, when suddenly an ad about Fiddler on the Roof caught his eye. The singer came to know that there was a show of the play. He was so thrilled that he would be getting to see his favorite actor perform right in front of him. He attended all the four shows of the play. Then he went backstage and introduced himself to Topol and took his autograph. Topol presented Kishore a copy of his autobiography titled *'Topol By Topol'*, and Kishore presented him a cassettes of his songs. According to Kishore *"Nobody can act the way Topol did in. Neither Dilip Kumar nor Ashok Kumar can do it"*.

Kishore lived a very romantic life and his quest for love led him getting married four times- every time to a beautiful woman of movies. He first got married to Ruma Devi, a leading actress of Bengali movies. From her, he had a son, Amit Kumar. Ruma was a talented actress. Kishore wanted her to be a housewife but she wanted to continue with her career, so the marriage couldn't survive. He then married Madhubala, the Venus of Indian screen. This marriage too couldn't last long since Madhubala was on the verge of death. Kishore fell madly in love with Madhubala while shooting for a film and his love got strong after marriage. After Madhubala's demise, Kishore had a marble grave built for her, where he used to light a lamp every evening. He sang many evergreen sad songs after her death. Madhubala's death left a deep impact on him wherein emerged the pain in Kishore's sad songs, which brought him everlasting fame.

His third marriage was with budding actress Yogita Bali. This marriage didn't last long, and ended in a divorce. Yogita later married actor Mithun Chakraborty. Kishore married again for the fourth time, to popular actress Leena Chandavarkar. Leena's first husband was shot dead and she was going through a tragic phase in life when she met the singer. When Kishore married Leena, he did not even think of becoming a father again as he was in his 50s. But he had another son from Leena, Sumeet Kumar, who was a source of immense joy to him. Kishore had always longed for a secure, happy family and it remained a dream until Leena came in his life. With her, he got emotional security.

Kishore was very fond of food. He loved eating thin Bengali style mutton curry with maida puris. He also liked gobi (cauliflower).

There was madness in the singer, which was obvious from umpteen incidents. It is said that he used to have a nameplate in the name of *Chhajju Ram* outside his bungalow in Mumbai. Whenever any stranger came to meet him, Kishore would reply *"Kishore ghar par nahin hain"* (Kishore is not at home). Kishore was very much particular about meeting people. He used to avoid meeting people without reason most of time.

Another interesting thing about Kishore is that he could come up with both, male and female voice. Once, Lata Mangeshkar was unable to come for the recording of the film *'Half Ticket'*, Kishore suggested to composer Sali Chowdhary that he would record in the female voice too. Salil thought that Kishore was joking, but took a chance knowing the imitating abilities of the singer, and finally Kishore sang in both voices brilliantly.

Though Kishore happened to be a big fan of Saigal and initially sang songs in Saigal's style, he later developed a style of his own. Kishore was often asked to sing songs in Saigal's style by the music directors. And they were willing to pay a good sum for that. But Kishore refused all those offers saying. *"Let Saigal be Saigal"*. He believed in originality, which is why he was a good singer, lyricist, composer, director and producer.

When Kishore passed away, composers were left holding tunes that they had composed only for Kishore and which they felt only he could have sung. Though many Kishore clones came up after his death, there has been no one like him. There are big singers in Bollywood today with good voices but they cannot be Kishore.

An incident about his singing stands out. Once R D Burman was composing the song *'Mere Naina Saawan Bhadon'* for *'Mehbooba'* and asked Kishore to sing it. It was a classical song but R D was determined to make Kishore sing it, knowing fully well that he was not a trained classical singer. Pancham Da was pretty sure that nobody except Kishore could sing it beautifully. Kishore lived up to his expectations and sang it remarkably. The song proved to be a mega hit. Apart from this, Kishore sang a number of other classical songs too.

Not many people know that in his entire life, Kishore did not smoke, drink and socialize. He was a nature-lover. He talked to trees, plants, water and birds. His love for natural surroundings led him to dig a canal around his bungalow, since he wanted to make his home look like one in Venice. People thought he was crazy because of all these antics but he was beyond people's thinking. While travelling in his car, new tunes would strike him and he used to hum it to his driver. And his driver's duty was to remember the tunes hum them back in the night to the singer. Kishore would then work on them.

The singer had always wanted to return to his native land Khandwa. His busy schedules and workload did not allow him to do that and his big desire remained a desire till he left the world. Forgetting this genius is impossible for his fans. Kishore said goodbye to the world on October 13, 1987. He recorded his last song for music director Bappi Lahri on October 12, 1987, a day before his death. His loss can never be fulfilled. Memories of Kishoreda are countless. His fans wish he was with them today.

****

2

Beware of Kishore Kumar – The Eccentric Behavior of the Legendary Singer

Kishore Kumar is still considered one of the finest and most successful singers in Bollywood. Although decades have passed since his death on 13th October 1987, the aroma and the magic of Kishore Kumar's singing could not be replaced by anyone in the singing world. The legendary singer's music is still fresh and is adored by today's generation. Apart from his music genius, the virtuoso of singing was quite famous rather notorious for his paranoid and eccentric behavior. Well, this often happened because of not getting paid by the producers in return of his services. Few incidents, which were reported during his lifetime, will be discussed in this column.

It was said that Kumar would sing only after the confirmation of payment from his secretary was received. On one occasion, when Kumar learnt that he was paid half for the movie he was roped in as an actor, he appeared on the sets with makeup placed on one side of his face. Seeing him when the director questioned, he replied *'Adha Paisa Tu Aadha Makeup (half makeup for half payment)'*.

On another incident, Kishore Kumar's eccentric behavior was witnessed. This is what happened that on the sets of *'Bhai Bhai'*, Kumar simply refused to act in the film since the director of the movie M V Raman owed the singer ☐ 5,000. Learning it, the elder brother Ashok Kumar insisted him to oblige the director. He went for the shooting and walked few steps and uttered to the director *'Paanch Hazaar Rupayaa (five thousand rupees)'*. Saying this, he reached at the end of the floor and then slipped from the set.

The singer had a soft heart for those who were kind to him. Apart from his principle of *'no money, no work'*, the music genius recorded songs for free for many producers even they were willing to pay him such as for the likes of superstar Rajesh Khanna and Danny Denzongpa. He even helped Bipin Gupta, the actor turned filmmaker, by giving him twenty thousand rupees for his movie *'Dal Mein Kaala (1964)'*.

There is another incident that describes the singer's humanity. Arun Kumar, the actor who first acknowledged and applauded Kishore Kumar's singing talent, in film industry, passed away. Kishore started sending money to his family regularly in Bhagalpur.

Kishore's another eccentric behavior was reported in the media. The legendary singer placed a sign *'Beware of Kishore Kumar'* at the door of his residence. The famous producer of Hindi film industry H.S.Rawail came to his home to pay his dues. After paying the dues, Rawail tried to

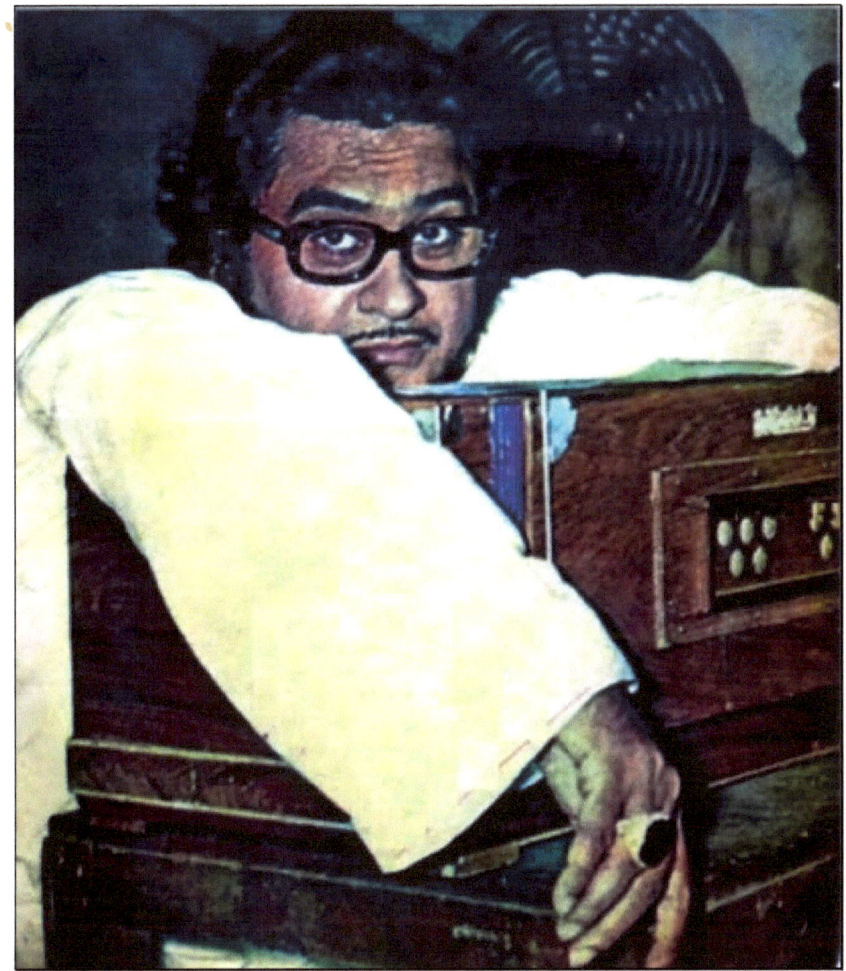
Kishore Kumar

shake hands with the singer, he took the producer's hand in his mouth, bit it and said *"Didn't you see what my signboard said?"*

On another reported incident, Kumar was signed to sing for famous filmmaker G.P.Sippy. By the time, Sippy reached Kumar's bungalow, he was out in his car. Seeing Sippy, he increased the speed of his vehicle despite filmmaker's asking him to stop. Sippy chased him until Kishore stopped his car near Madh Fort. When the filmmaker questioned him about his weird behavior, Kumar simply refused recognizing him and instead warned him to call the police. Next morning, Kishore reached at the recording studio, the angry producer asked about the yesterday's incident, Kishore straightly said that Sippy must have seen a dream because he was in Khandwa yesterday.

A producer got a decree from the court that the singer must follow the orders of his director. On an incident later, Kishore came on the set and did not come out of his car until the director asked him to do so.

A director was filming a car scene in Bombay (now Mumbai), the director forgot to say *'cut'*, and Kishore drove the car until he reached Khandala.

On Kalidas Batyabbal's report, the income tax raided Kishore Kumar's bungalow. Later, the singer invited Kalidas at his residence and asked Batyabbal to enter in the cupboard to show him something inside. When he entered into the cupboard, he locked it and Kalidas remained there for almost two hours.

The singer was isolated and called himself *'loner'*. In an interview to a journalist, he revealed that he preferred talking to his trees. He also introduced the journalist with the trees by their names at his bungalow and said they were his close friends.

Despite all these eccentric behaviors of the singer, Kishore Kumar was loveable and will remain the same forever for his fans.

****

3

Gulzar – the Man Whose Creativity Knows No Limits

Although I used to watch Gulzar Saab's movies when I was child, but the first time I got introduced with the creative genius was in early 90s era. Gulzar Saab was the central talk of the literary circles of Urdu where I used to sit since I also belonged to the world of literature apart from my Bollywood journalism profession. The people who inspired me in life were his fans and they all the time talked big about this super genius who always focused the ordinary things and common people in particular in his creations. Gulzar is the one who makes ordinary things special – the things we most of the time ignore by not giving them importance. He is amongst those people who spiritually mesmerized me, inspired me and simply stole me from tip to toe.

I remember the night way back in early 90s time when a friend of mine, who I respect like an elder brother, asked the music shop owner to play the song *'Tujhse Naraz Nahi Zindagi'* in full volume. The requester was in a sad and depressed state of mind and wanted to do catharsis with this song. Both of us were standing outside the shop and Lata Ji was singing with much zeal and in her usual magical brilliance in the background on Gulzar Saab's beautiful and heart-touching poetic lines composed by another music virtuoso late R.D Burman that we both stood still as if we were lifeless. The moment was magical and I still can visualize it and see the big circles of smoke coming out of our puffing of cigarettes. Almost for around 8 to 10 times, the shop owner had to play the song repeatedly since we were not in a mood to let him play any other track. From that day on, this track has become one of my hot favorite songs. Whether I feel low or am in a happy state of mind, this number spells magic with me.

There will be hardly any movie left which I have not watched churned out by Gulzar Ji. Even I have watched his TV serials many a time including his most popular one – *'Mirza Ghalib'*. His books too are in my collection just like his movies. *'Dastkhat'* and *'Chand Pukhraj Ka'* are the books I have read a number of times. *'Zikr Jehlum Ka Ho Baat Ho Deny Ki, Chand Pukhraj Ka Raat Pashminy Ki'*....'wow'!

When Gulzar wrote the everlasting and evergreen song *'Mera Kuch Saaman'* for the movie *'Ijaazat'*, he took it to his best buddy Pancham Da (R.D. Burman) for the composition. Reading the song, Burman straightly refused Gulzar saying *"tomorrow you will ask me to compose the headlines of Times of India"*. Pancham found it meter-less and out of composition. This depressed the lyricist, but the same day at night around 2:30 a.m., Burman was right there outside Gulzar's home. He was so excited and kept his hand on horn button. The moment Gulzar Saab came into his balcony, Burman asked him to immediately come to his car. While driving, he was constantly beating the dashboard to generate the tune for *'Mera Kuch Saaman'*.

The prodigy had arranged the tune for the song. Once it was composed and out, it shook the music scene and added more values to Gulzar Saab's already established career. The song today is called 'timeless'.

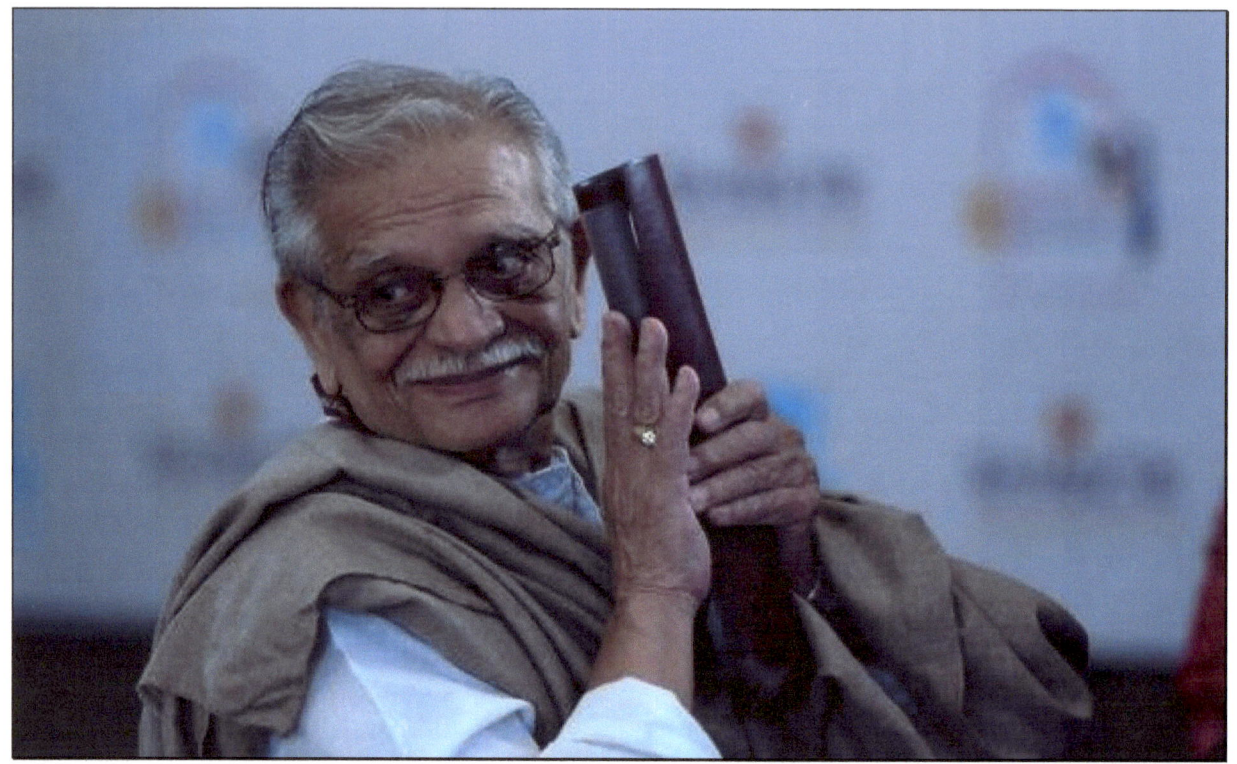

Gulzar

Not many know that Gulzar learnt the meter of Urdu poetry from renowned late Pakistani poet and litterateur Ahmad Nadeen Qasmi whom he used to call *'Baba'*. He also shares a very good relationship with Qasmi Sahib's family.

Jhelum, a Pakistani city in the region of Punjab, is very close to his heart and this is because Gulzar was born in Dina, District Jhelum. And in his creative works, he mentions *'Dina'* and *'Jhelum'* a lot. About his date of birth, he says that parents never used to note down the date of birth of the kids when he was born therefore he is not sure about his exact birthdate.

Gulzar was born to Sikh family and was named Sampooran Singh Karla. Hardly any people know that Gulzar converted to Islam because of Meena Kumari who he loved the most. It is said that while she was still in Kamal Amrohi's nikah, she and Gulzar came close to each other. Meena (Mahjabeen Bano) was Muslim like her husband Kamal (Syed Amir Haider Kamal Naqvi) and she used to say prayers even on the sets. It is also mentioned that she used to recite Quran after her arrival on the sets – this impressed Gulzar Saab a lot. Mahjabeen was very stick to fasting and when she was in the hospital, Gulzar fasted on her behalf (according to media reports). There are other reports as well which suggest that due to his love for Sufism, he developed liking for the religion Islam.

Bollywood Diary *Goher Iqbal Punn*

In an interview with Dunya TV of Pakistan, when the host of the show visited Gulzar Saab at his residence in Mumbai, the host asked *'Are you Muslim?'* To answer this question, Gulzar said *'kya apko mery Musalman hony py shaq hai?'* (Do you have any doubt of my being a Muslim?). To a question *'Does he still fast?'* he replied *'I fast for the whole month of Ramdan, but now due to being old, he often misses fasting'*.

No matter whatever his religion is, the thing that matters he is simply loveable. *"Iss more sy jaaty hain kuch sust kadam rasty kuch tez kadam rahein"*...simply magical – only a creative poet who loves nature can write it. Hats off to you Gulzar Saab – you are a legend Bollywood and Urdu literature have ever produced!

****

4

The Hidden Love Story of Reena Roy and Mohsin Khan – Jaya Bachchan's Role in Helping Her Decide for the Pakistani Cricketer

Reena Roy and Mohsin Khan's marriage was much-talked about and the central focus of India and Pakistan when the two tied the nuptial knot way back in 1983. Both were at the peak of their respective careers when they decided to settle down in life – Reena was the leading Bollywood actress and Mohsin was the top batsman of Pakistan cricket team. They were enjoying their careers and were in massive demand with big fan following. One of the higher-paid actresses of her time, Reena (born Saira Ali) was madly in love with actor Shatrughan Sinha (her costar in many movies) before Mohsin came into her life. But after the arrival of Khan into Roy's glamorous life, she was nonetheless in a confused state of mind whether to be the better half of Sinha or Khan. Reena was on a constant see-saw, as Shatru was also shaky to make his final decision since he too had lost his heart to his childhood sweetheart Poonam Sinha – who was crowned Miss Young India in 1968. Poonam appeared in Hindi movies as well in minor roles before her marriage to Sinha. It is believed that the marriage of Shatru and Poonam in 1980 paved way for Reena Roy to marry her dream man Mohsin Hassan Khan.

Roy was much depressive those days because at one side it was the leading actor of Hindi cinema Shatrughan Sinha and on the other was Mohsin Khan – the charming, suave, internationally popular handsome cricketer of Pakistan. It was late Bollywood actor Vinod Khanna, who took her out of this phase. And on the other hand, Jaya Bachchan (Bollywood actress and the wife of legendary actor Amitabh Bachchan) helped Reena say 'yes' to the marriage proposal of the Pakistani cricketer whom Roy loved head to toe, but was reluctant to finalize her decision. Once she decided to toss away Sinha from her life, it was the moment to let happiness come in her depressed life. The leading Bollywood actress had decided to say 'goodbye' to her successful film career to play the 'perfect bahu' (perfect daughter-in-law) of Pakistan.

Reena's love for Mohsin had crossed all the boundaries and the lovebirds were the headlines of all the tabloids and newspapers in India, Pakistan and across the globe. Paparazzi were always behind the two to get the juicy tidbits. Reena was often found in the stadium whenever Mohsin was playing the match. Both were unable to detach – it was Heer-Ranjha love saga, which was going on rapidly. Whenever India won the match from Pakistan, entire Bollywood industry would say 'Jhal Gaye Reena Roy' (Reena Roy got jealous). Khan was her prince charming and she used to dream as if he was galloping to her sitting on a horse.

By the time she was in London for a show of Amitabh Bachchan, Khan went there to meet her to spend quality time together. He would call her in the evenings and the two then would go for long drives. The two used to exchange their professions, parents, ambitions and future. Long dating of almost six years cemented a powerful relationship of love between them.

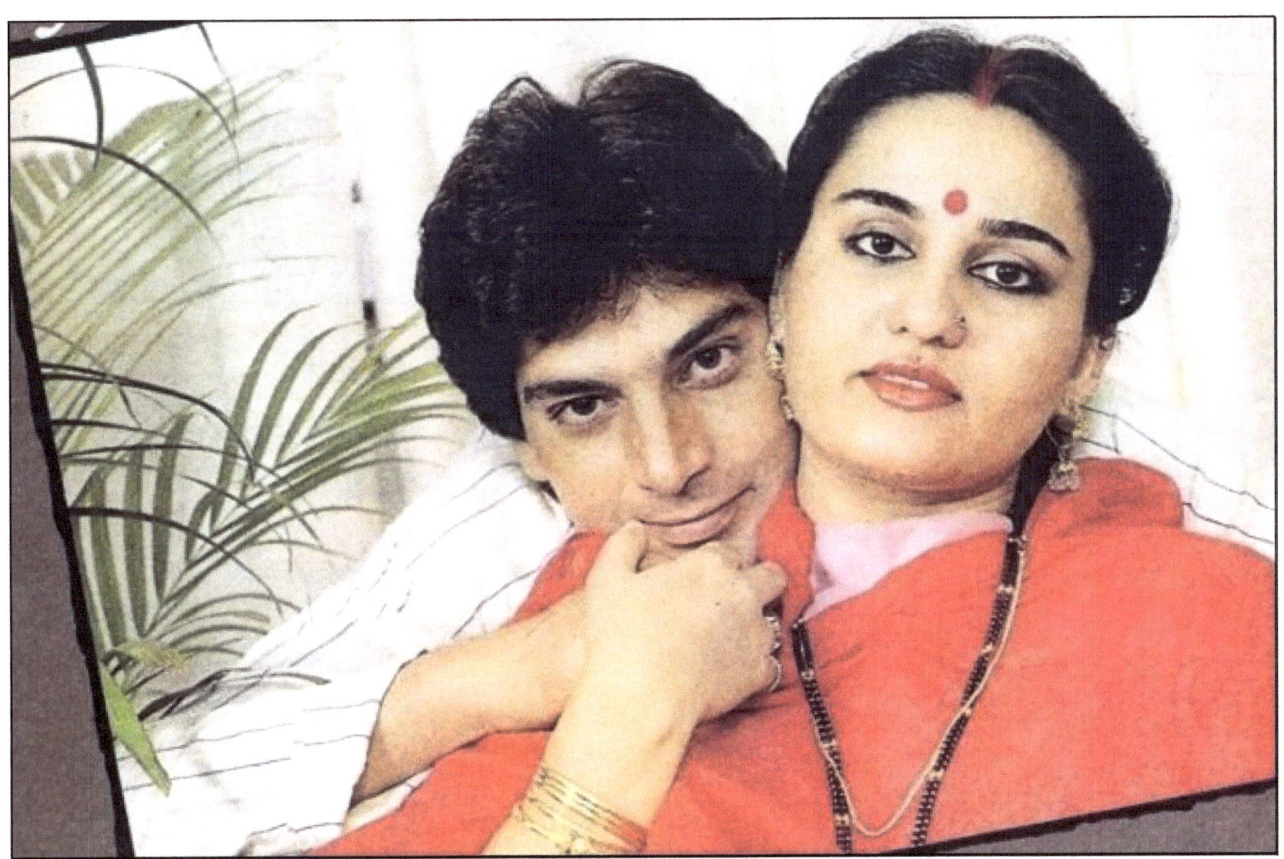

Reena Roy and Mohsin Hassan Khan

When Mohsin was not with her and was away for his game in different parts of the world, the actress missed him a lot and finally confessed her mad love for the Pakistani cricketer to her close friend Jaya Bachchan. It was Jaya who went ahead of helping Reena to put all her doubts for her family, her career and about Shatrughan Sinha. She asked her to find her own identity. Jaya let Reena Roy to make decision to marry Khan, as the two were in a relationship with more than six years. She helped her realize that he had everything such as talents, success, fame and money. Roy had earned a big fame, stardom and money by then and had spent a long innings in the filmdom. Now it was the time to think for her personal life. Jaya made her understand the fact that if she missed the chance, she would never probably get another in life. She made up her mind at last, as Mohsin was her ultimate dream guy she wanted to have as a life partner.

For the actress who always lived in a fantasy world, it was a quiet wedding on 1st April, 1983. The top notch actress of Hindi film industry at the height of her fame quit movies to be happy in her upcoming married life with her prince charming. Industry made fun of her and costars laughed at her, but the adamant actress tied the knot leaving all and sundry behind and flew to her new home - Karachi, Pakistan. Reena Roy and Mohsin Khan's marriage hogged the light since both were superstars in their own trades and had biggest fan following. Years later, the two divorced. Mohsin remarried a girl in Pakistan and their (Mohsin and Reena's) daughter's custody was given to Reena Roy. She was named 'Jannat' (heaven) by Mohsin Khan, but later her name was changed to Sanam by Reena Roy and her sister Barkha. Heer-Ranjha love eventually melted down with the divorce. Once passionate lovers became strangers to each other – divorce drifted them apart.

****

5

Salman Khan Slapped Katrina Kaif in Public, Pushed Aishwarya Rai and Smashed a Bottle on Somy Ali's Head

The anger of Salman Khan is known by all. It has also become a part of his personality. The brawny Khan keeps display the same whenever he is out. Apart from the abundant amount of controversies, Salman is all the time laced with, he has also faced a number of domestic violence hullabaloos. Not only Salman Khan, but also many other Bollywood celebrities have been involved in domestic violence. Khan has reportedly done so with his girlfriends.

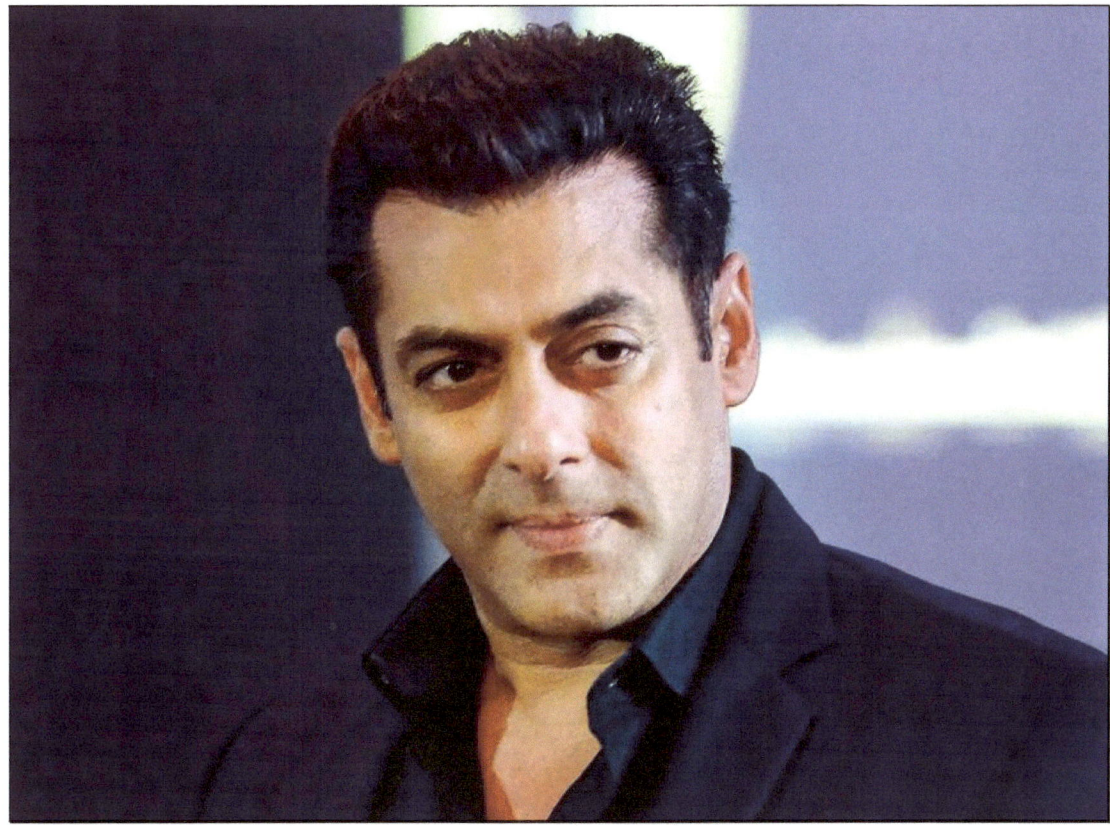

Salman Khan

His previous girlfriend Aishwarya Rai was abused by him. Reports exhibit that Salman had become alcoholic and would become abusive when he used to drink. In 2000, Aishwarya and her parents had filed a complaint against Salman Khan. Shah Rukh Khan's produced movie 'Chalte Chalte' took Aishwarya initially on board as a leading actress, but due to Salman's hotheaded and nasty behavior with Rai on the sets, Shah Rukh had to replace Aishwarya with Rani Mukerji. One of the incidents on the sets happened when Salman Khan pushed Asihwarya Rai on the floor. He then hit Aishwarya's car while he was leaving the set. This became unbearable for King Khan, which resulted in Rai's dropping from the cast.

Somy Ali, Bollywood's actress of 90s, was Salman Khan's girlfriend then. She too faced the violence by the macho Khan. On a film's set, Salman emptied the bottle of Thumps Up on her head. Sources claimed that later Salman smashed the bottle on Somy's head that she received injuries and had to go for first aid.

Katrina Kaif, Salman Khan's girlfriend who he cannot forget even today after the breakup, was also the victim of Khan's violence. Once after some arguments between the two, Salman got massively angry and threw all of her shampoo bottles out of her home. During another argument session between the lovers while they were having dinner in a restaurant in Mumbai, Salman could not control on his anger and slapped Kaif on her face. This was truly a big humiliation which Katrina Kaif could not bear. On the sets of Kabir Khan's Ek Tha Tiger, Salman allegedly hit Katrina Kaif because she was clad in a tight dress, which was revealing her body parts. Reports suggest that this behavior of Salman proved to be the reason of breakup between the two.

Sources assert that Salman's anger and abusing turned out to be the reasons for his breakups and because of this no woman sticks to his life.

****

6

Anu Malik Drove into a Dark Empty Place and Unzipped His Pants and Asked Me to: Bollywood Singer

Bollywood is always echoed with casting couch stories and sexual favors, which many celebrities have claimed to be part of. We often hear stories of sexual harassments at work places, but Bollywood – our own glittering colossal entertainment industry too is filled up with abundant of sagas relating to this evil practice which has started gaining strength now. Anu Malik, coveted music composer, from the outset has been under mammoth controversies of sexual harassment and even he had to face the music when popular songstress Alisha Chinai dragged him to the court for sexual harassment allegation in 90s era. Alisha accused him of molestation charges. Chinai revealed in the media that she was molested by Mailk during the making of her hit track *'Made in India'*. Other popular female singers such as Sona Mohapatra, Neha Bhasin, Caralisa Monteiro and Shweta Pandit too have come up to raise their voice against the musician's predatory behavior. Alisha, famous Indian pop and playback singer, rubbed her shoulders with all the female singers who built a strong voice against the composer saying *"Every word said and written about Anu Malik is true. I stand by all the women who have finally spoken up. May they find peace and closure in their lives."*

Shweta, popular Bollywood vocalist, shared her experience on Twitter naming it the 'worst memory' of her life saying it was year 2000 when she got her break as a lead singer in *'Mohabbatein'*. Yash Raj Films' movie gave her 5 songs to sing after she auditioned for the final selection among several singers. She was merely 14 at that time. To follow up with the success of the soundtracks she rendered in the film album, she needed to have more songs to keep pace with the instant success. She got a call from Malik's then manager Mustafa to come to meet the musician at Empire Studio in Andheri, Mumbai. It was 2001 and Pandit got thrilled as all newcomers would be. She along with his mother stepped into the studio where Anu Malik was recording a song with Sunidhi Chauhan and Shaan for the film *'Awara Pagal Deewana'*. Malik wanted to hear her voice, thus asked her to sing the title song for the film 'Har Dil Jo Pyar Karega' as a voice test. Being a splendid singer, Shweta sang it with conviction that impressed the composer and he could not help praising her voice. The composer said to Pandit *"I will give you this song along with Sunidhi and Shaan but first give me a kiss now."* She was just 15 at that time and felt like someone had just stabbed her into her stomach. Shweta used to call her 'Anu Uncle', as he knew her family for decades.

Sona Mohapatra, one of the leading voices of Bollywood brigade, raised big voice on social platform such as Facebook and Instagram against the sexual predating of the music scorer. Mohapatra, in October 2018, accused not only Anu Malik but also singer Kailash Kher of sexual misconduct. Unzipping an incident involving Kailash, Sona uttered that once the singer placed his hand on her thigh and said *"you are so beautiful, feel so good that a musician (her husband composer Ram Sampath) got you not an actor."* Sharing another incident of this kind, Mohapatra revealed that during a live concert, Kailash asked her to skip the soundcheck and join him in his room to *'catch up'*.

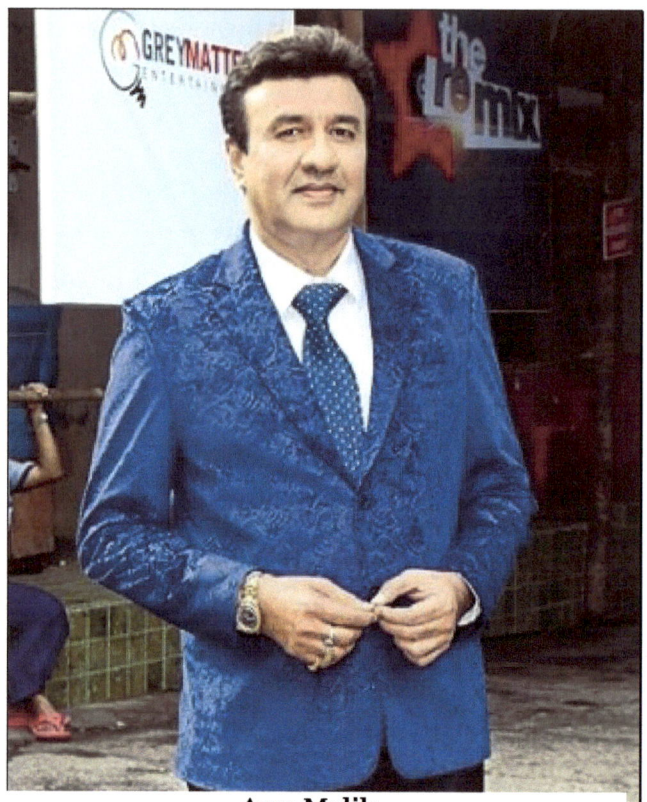

Anu Malik

Sona, in her accusations against Malik and Kher, also accused Anu of passing a lecherous comment in presence of her husband. Mohapatra then also revealed that the composer would call her in odd hours asking her awkward questions.

Playback singer Sona Mohapatra was asked to leave Sa Re Ga Ma Pa, a reality show on which she was a judge because she provided Anu Malik publicity by raising her voice against his sexual predating and her actions took up TRPs of the rival TV show.

Malik had to leave the judge seat of the Indian Idol 10 after sexual harassments accusations emerged from all corners. But when he returned to the following season of the show in its 11th edition, Sona said *"the sexual predator is back on the same seat"*.

Joining in the bandwagon of the voices raised by the female singers against the sexual misconduct of the music composer, coveted playback vocalist Neha Bhasin accused of Malik of sexual pestering in a series of tweets. Malik's return to the singing show as a judge in its 11th season set many on fire and it made the victims angry such as the likes of Sona Mohapatra, Shweta Pandit and Neha Bhasin. Neha uncovered the incident in which Anu Malik laid on a couch in front of her in a sexual style and praised for her eyes. She said she was just 21 when this incident took place. She further wrote in her tweet that she fled from the scene lying that her mother was waiting outside. Bhasin also said that Anu even later messaged and called her to which she stopped responding.

Caralisa Monteiro, best known for songs like *'Dard-e-Disco'*, *'Mitwa'* and *'Nashe Si Chadh Gayi'* also came up sharing her experience with Malik saying he insisted her to come to his house for a jam session, but since she was uncomfortable with him, she refused to turn up.

Two more anonymous women, who did not want their identities to be revealed, came up with their shocking experiences against the sexual harassment of the composer. An inspiring female singer told to the media that she met Malik in 1990 at Mehboob Studios. He rubbed against the vocalist and then apologized for his misbehavior. But soon he started behaving worse. Once she was at his home, he sat next to her on the sofa (his family was not at home). He lifted her skirt and dropped his pants. She tried to push him back and rushed out to the door, but he was too strong to hold her. Luckily for her, someone rang the bell and she slipped away instantly from his home. Later, he threatened the woman and asked her not to tell anyone of the incident. One day, while he was dropping her home, Anu again sexually harassed the girl in a deserted area. According to the singer, it was around 8:30 p.m. when Malik drove into a dark empty place. He unzipped his pants and asked her to lick him. The female singer told him 'no' and urged him to let her go. Instead, Malik pulled her hair and stuffed her face in his lap and abused her. A guard out there approached to the car, it gave the singer courage to escape.

Another vocalist spoke of a meeting with Anu Malik taken place in a studio where he asked the singer to come wearing a chiffon saree next time. Upon learning that the girl had no boyfriend, the composer hugged her tightly. On realizing that the recording studio was sound proof, she pushed him away and said that he was happy with his wife and a sensitive man. This budding singer later refused participating in Indian Idol Season 10 when she got to know about Anu Malik on a judge seat.

Many from the industry came up in support of Malik such as Hema Sardesai, Sonu Nigam, Vishal Dadlani and Neha Kakkar. On the other hand, Anu's lawyer also denied all allegations terming them false and baseless.

The truth has to be taken out whatever it is. On the other hand, the fact remains that Bollywood is laced with such activities like sexual harassments, sexual favors and casting couch. Many newcomers obey the demands and the others (who don't) raise their voice.

****

7

You Need to Give Sexual Favors If You Want to Get Big Break in Bollywood

Bollywood – the largest entertainment industry of the world exists in the financial hub of Mumbai, which is called 'The City of Dreams'. The industry lures the eyes of almost everyone whoever loves watching Hindi movies and many of them pack the bags and head to the city to make their dreams come true. Few of them make their mark in the industry and the rest takes the route back to their homes with utter disappointment. Bollywood charms everyone. The big stardom, success, wealth, lavish lifestyle, respect and the perks conferred upon you when you are a celebrity – all catch your heart. This is Bollywood – the Hindi cinema industry. My association with this industry dates back to 2002 when I first wrote a cover story on the late legendary singer Kishore Kumar for the much popular film magazine Screen (an entertainment magazine by Indian Express which also holds Star Screens Awards every year) and it was well-received and liked by his fans, Bollywood aficionados and even the Editor that I could not help being a part of this genre of journalism. Apart from the sparkles and attractions Bollywood is endowed with, the industry often suffers accusations and this appears like a scar on its face.

Sexual harassment is found everywhere and the Hindi cinema industry is no exception at all. The media is always abuzz about the allegations of sexual harassments on Bollywood celebrities. It is not new for Bollywood rather it has been with the fraternity since the beginning. But since last decade or so, the noise for sexual harassment is quite high in the fraternity that feeds the tabloids with enough dose of spicy content to adorn their pages. Whenever any report related to this issue comes up, the entire media begins buzzing and all eyes get focused on the news leads. Years back in 2005, when the casting couch reports on Bollywood's leading villain Shakti Kapoor hit the media, the industry shook heavily since it was an explosive sting operation done by India TV in which the leading villain was filmed to ask for the sexual favors from an undercover reporter posing as an upcoming actress in a hotel room in Mumbai. This sting operation was undoubtedly the biggest controversy of Hindi cinema industry that revealed Kapoor's off-screen villainous side. When questioned about his role in propositioning the undercover reporter, Shakti claimed that she has threatened to commit suicide if he did not visit her hotel room. Even he was also heard saying that the girl (reporter) threatened to kill him if he did not come to meet her in hotel. The entire Indian media was jam-packed with breaking news and controversies formulated around this sting operation. The actor found no escaping at all since he got entangled in the same.

Shakti Kapoor received mammoth criticism for dragging into and involving the big names of the industry in the messy act. He was also filmed naming industry's most popular names who he claimed had slept their way to success. He claimed in the clip that everyone had to sleep 'once' with the bigwigs of the industry to get the big break. Shakti unzipped it to the undercover reporter in the video that Aishwarya Rai (Bollywood's leading actress and former Miss World) doled sexual favors to popular filmmaker Subhash Ghai for the leading role in 'Taal' (released in 1999) – the movie which then changed Rai's career altogether by soaring her film career to sky high and she was also nominated for Filmfare Best Actress Award for the movie. Before 'Taal', Aishwarya was consistently giving flops. Earlier Mahima Choudhary and Manisha Koirala had also claimed that Ghai asked for the sexual favors to give them the big breaks in Bollywood.

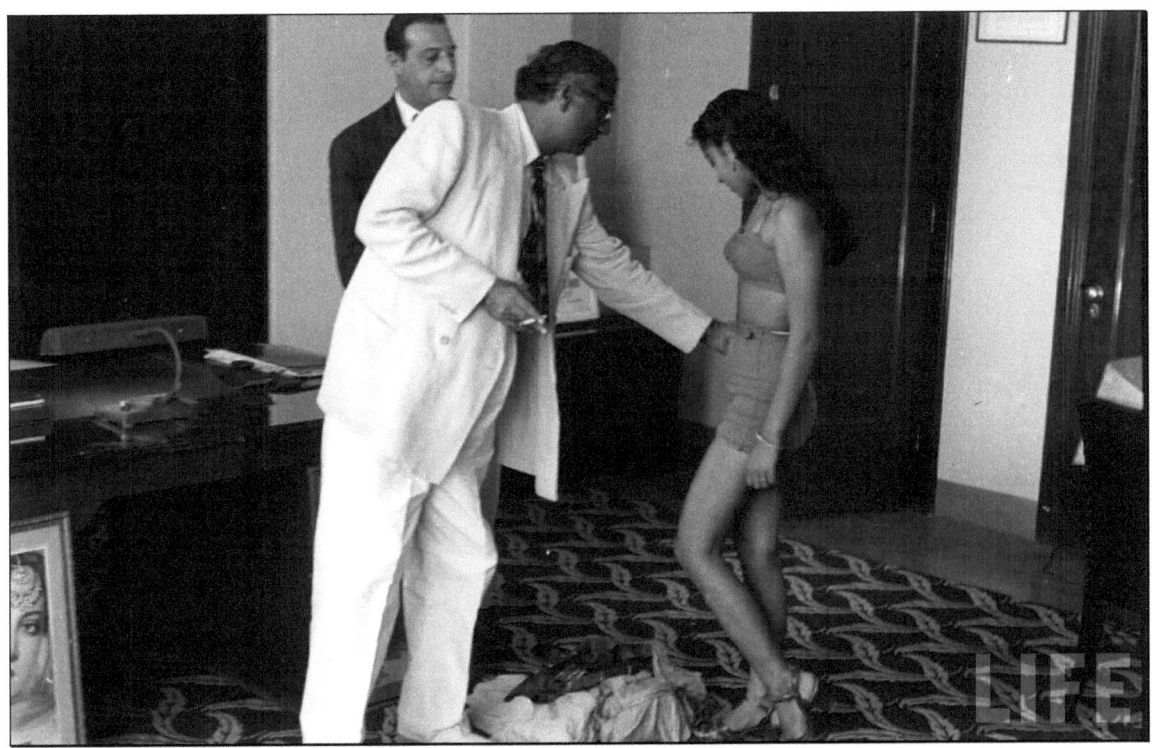

Sexual Favors

Kapoor also dragged actresses Preity Zinta and Rani Mukerji's names in the video claiming that they also underwent sexual favors to make big in cinema industry. Shakti denied all reports and the videos making rounds in the media naming them 'doctored and tampered'. Film and TV Producers' Guild banned the actor by not working with him anymore. The actor then had to apologize to the actresses and other industry people whose names he revealed in the video clip.

Post the claims of Shakti Kapoor involving him and Aishwarya Rai and then the claims made by Mahima and Manisha's to bed with him for big roles, Subhash Ghai was again accused of rape in 2018. An anonymous woman alleged him that he spiked her drink and then sexually assaulted her in a hotel room. The woman did not want to be named, as she was a credible media personality which was why her name was not revealed in reports. According to her, the director would often call her to his home for script sessions. The actress then claimed that Ghai forcefully kissed her once on the set. She narrated the rape incident that at a late music session

Ghai offered her a drink that was spiked and while he was dropping her to her home in his car, he took her to a hotel room and assaulted her before she lost her conscious.

Saloni Chopra, another Bollywood actress, accused director Sajid Khan of sexual harassment while she worked with him as an assistant. A female journalist also put the same accusations on the filmmaker revealing that she went to interview her at his sister Farah Khan's home when he forcefully kissed her.

Shiney Ahuja, a famed film actor, spent three months in prison after he was accused of raping his domestic servant. Renowned actress Renuka Shahane too shared her past account of sexual harassment in the media. She was once staying in a hotel room for a film shooting, where a hotel staffer came to her room and laid out the food. He started praising her claiming him as her biggest fan. While talking to her, he started masturbating in front of her. Renuka then shouted and asked him to leave the room. There are plenty of other incidents relating to this bitter fact and if I start writing on, the story will begin multiplying the pages.

This is the Hindi cinema industry where you have to pay the price to make your name no matter if you have talents – all matters is a 'chance' and that is provided with a price. This is the bitter side of Bollywood which cannot be overlooked.

****

8

When a Famous Bollywood Film Director Had to Sleep with a Widely Popular Film Producer to Get His Bollywood Break

Casting Couch in Bollywood – well, you must be aware of this terminology, as a lot has been written and is discussed on it in the media and over social media. Bollywood is a giant entertainment industry of the world. One may stumble upon favorism and lobbyism over there, but they seem okay because this kind of practice prevails in our societies and businesses and we are used to them. But the evil practice of 'casting couch' does not seem fine and cannot be approved of. Although it must have been there in Hindi cinema industry from the outset, but I remember in early 2000s quite a big noise was raised in media. Following to it, a number of scandals came up involving many a big names of the industry. Big hullabaloo kept going on and then silence overcame, as usually it happens with every issue in the media.

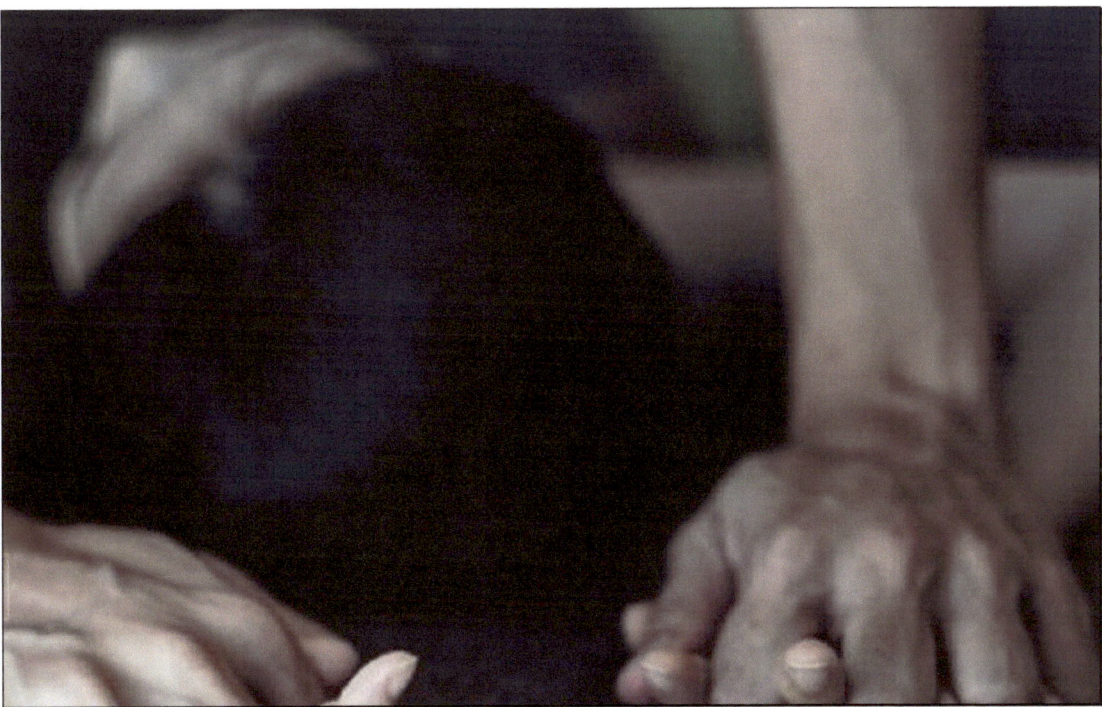

Casting Couch in Bollywood

In simple words, casting couch is a trade in which sexual favors are given for a role or work in movies. Where a number of stars were dragged into the matter, few also opened up by spilling the beans. Even in recent years, few known actresses of Bollywood industry revealed the facts that they had to obey for the sexual business in order to get a chance in films.

The most alarming thing, which I had come to know from a friend in Bollywood (who is a model-actress) during mid-2000, was the existence of male homosexuality in the film fraternity. The fact she disclosed to me was simply surprising at least for me because the persons involved were among those celebrities of Hindi film industry I used to admire a lot. Well, what she revealed to me was that she once approached to a renowned film director for work, who was once a film critic and entertainment journalist prior to entering into Bollywood. He asked her to meet him over dinner cum champagne in a private room at a five star hotel. It was a clear indication of casting couch – the sexual favor in return for work in his film. When the actress turned down his offer, he told her that this was a trade in which all aspiring actors had to undergo – the give and take business. The director also revealed her that he too had to sleep with the widely famous producer (who was the son of the very big name of Bollywood industry and had the big production house) to get his break in filmdom – to direct a movie. Both names – the director and producer simply shook me from tip to toe since I was an admirer of that director and the fan of the movies of that producer being a movie critic and Bollywood journalist.

Before writing this column on the sensitive issue of casting couch in Bollywood, I first thought of revealing the names of these two persons. But since I do not belong to dirty journalism and dislike gutter press, I skipped the idea and protected their identification. I too have been a part of Bollywood for last many years through my journalistic works, and I like to see this industry flourishing in a clean manner. I admit that stars' kids always have a safe place to enter in film business and do not encounter these kinds of situations. On the contrary the others have to undergo and face casting couch. For newcomers and outsiders, the formula is simple – sell your body and get a chance in return. It is quite difficult to overcome this dirty business, but raising the voice and bringing the facts in media can at least make a difference.

****

9

Are Journalists the Representatives of the Celebrities?

There is a notion in society and even it is often said in many circles that journalists are the representatives of the celebrities when it comes to their role of providing the news to the masses. There is no denying in mentioning that journalists act as a bridge between the celebrities and common people and this is because they endow the people with the news about the celebrities. Since celebrities are public properties, thus whatever happens in their lives particularly in their official lives need to be covered to convey to the masses. Yes, to some extent, one might coin the term 'representation' of the celebs for the journalists, but calling them actual 'representative' is simply wrong. Since the journalists, by performing their duties, take the factual news from the celebrities and convey them to the masses for their information, thus in this regard, it could be termed 'representation'. But on the other hand, if it is stated that they transmit the news to the people according to what a celebrity dictates or narrates to them to publish, it is plainly 'no'. If it is done, 'yes', it is called a 'representation' then. I clearly admit that yellow journalism exists in our surroundings.

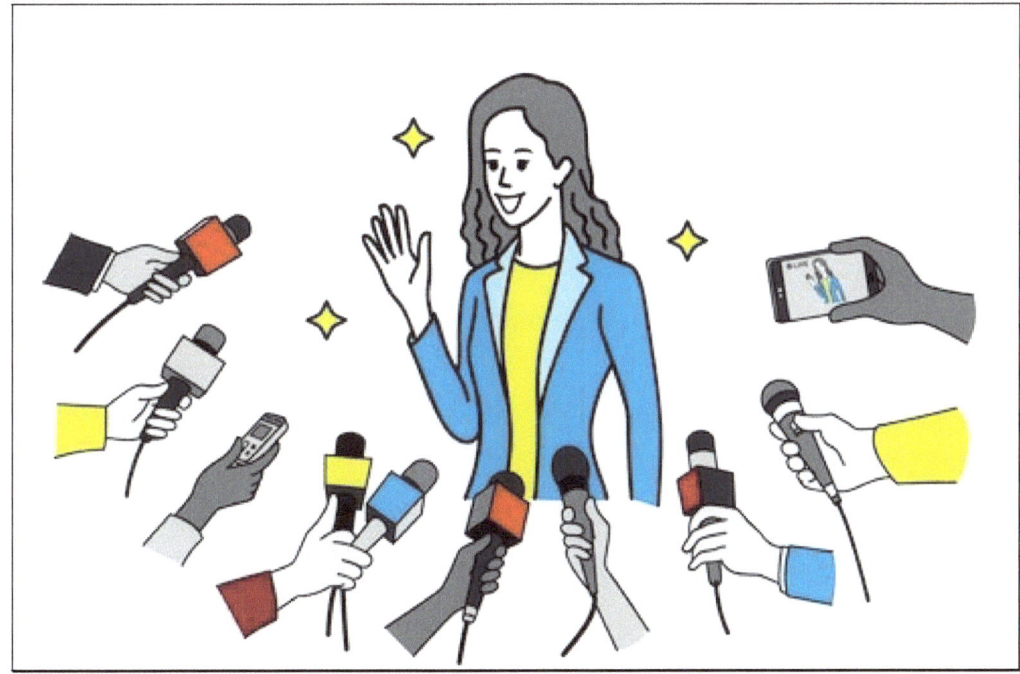

Journalists and Celebrities

There are

journalists whose bread and butter or their extra income sources come from 'gutter journalism' (I term it 'gutter journalism', as it is simply a dirty act that unfortunately prevails in this profession with whom I am also associated) and they can openly be called 'the representatives of celebrities'. But in general, I can amenably say that 'we', the journalists are NOT the representatives of the luminaries – we are out there in the field to find the truth and grab the news using our trustworthy sources.

Few years back, I was watching a talk show on an Indian television where the host had invited both the celebrities from Bollywood and entertainment journalists on the show. The topic of the show was the same on which I am writing this column. I do not want to name the celebrities and the journalists but all of them were high profiles. The celebs were of the view that the journalists were their representatives as they conveyed to the people whatever we did and endowed them with. According to them, the journalists took the center position between them and their fans (general public) and because of them, their lives and work were conveyed to the people. On the contrary, the group of journalists kept denying the celebrities' claims. I agree, the journalists do take the central position and because of their role, the news about the luminaries reach out to the people, but calling them 'representative' is a wrong terminology and this was what being churned out by the bunch of journalists on the show.

Well, if I am not wrong – the actual representatives of the celebrities are their public relation managers, as they represent them in the media by providing them the stories and press releases about their works. To cut it short, a true journalist is the one who finds factual stories and publishes it without any bias. Representation is another job not journalism.

****

10

Does Pakistan Need Bollywood?

No denying in saying that Pakistani artists have been doing great in Bollywood and have earned big names in return of their contributions to the world's second largest entertainment industry. With a tag of a Bollywood celebrity or having a Bollywood experience to their credit, these Pakistani artists are now earning quite handsome amount in their own homeland - Pakistan. And, yes, the drowning Pakistani entertainment fraternity is willing to pay whatever is demanded by these Bollywood stars. But 'why' they are being paid high when the industry is falling down and needs boost up? Well, the straight answer is very clear - Lollywood and even the entire Pakistani entertainment fraternity need their support to stand up. Cinema industry in Pakistan, which once was flourishing decades back, has started its revival procedure. And in this process, Bollywood returned Pakistani artists have been stretching their hands for its support.

With a Bollywood tag, they are now treated with utter respect and their recognition is much higher than other brigade of Pakistani stars. Sensing this importance, they do not leave any stone unturned to encash their worth. From Rahat Fateh Ali Khan to Atif Aslam to Adnan Sami Khan or even to others like Shafqat Amanant Ali Khan - all have proved their mettle on Hindi entertainment soil. Today, their demands are acknowledged with respect. Recently Rahat Fateh Ali Khan, internationally renowned playback and qawwali singer, was conferred with an honorary doctorate degree by Oxford University. The Sufi Qawwal and vocalist also enjoys a good rapport with international stars and bigwigs of the world. This all is due to Bollywood. The stardom Bollywood has endowed him could not have been possible being attached with Pakistani entertainment industry. His Bollywood songs soared his popularity graph to such heights that today he is supremely successful and one of the highest paid singers in India and Pakistan. The like of Mukesh Ambani sends his private jet to fetch the singer to perform at his parties. Many other perks like these, Rahat relishes with and the credit goes to Hindi filmdom which made him the star. Today not only he but also all other Bollywood returned Pakistani stars are packed with handsome amount of works with colossal pay cheques. These stars should not be termed Bollywood returned in actual since they still work in the giant entertainment industry to intact their international stardom.

Although Pakistani artists have been showing their prowess in Bollywood since the outset such as ghazal singer Ghulam Ali, Nazia Hassan (late), Reshma (late), Ustad Nusrat Fateh Ali Khan (late) to many others, but the junk that turned to Bollywood started in early 2000 when the leading actor Jawed Shaikh paved way to others to join Hindi cinema brigade. Starred in merely minor roles, this leading Pakistani actor got the Bollywood tag to further boost his career graph in Lollywood and the man succeeded. The same goes for the likes of Atif Aslam (who has been doing well in Bollywood playback singing), Shafqat Amanat Ai Khan and others. Even Ali Zafar, whose career drowned after instant popularity in Pakistan, started making his public relationing there and got work. Now he is well-reputed in his homeland.

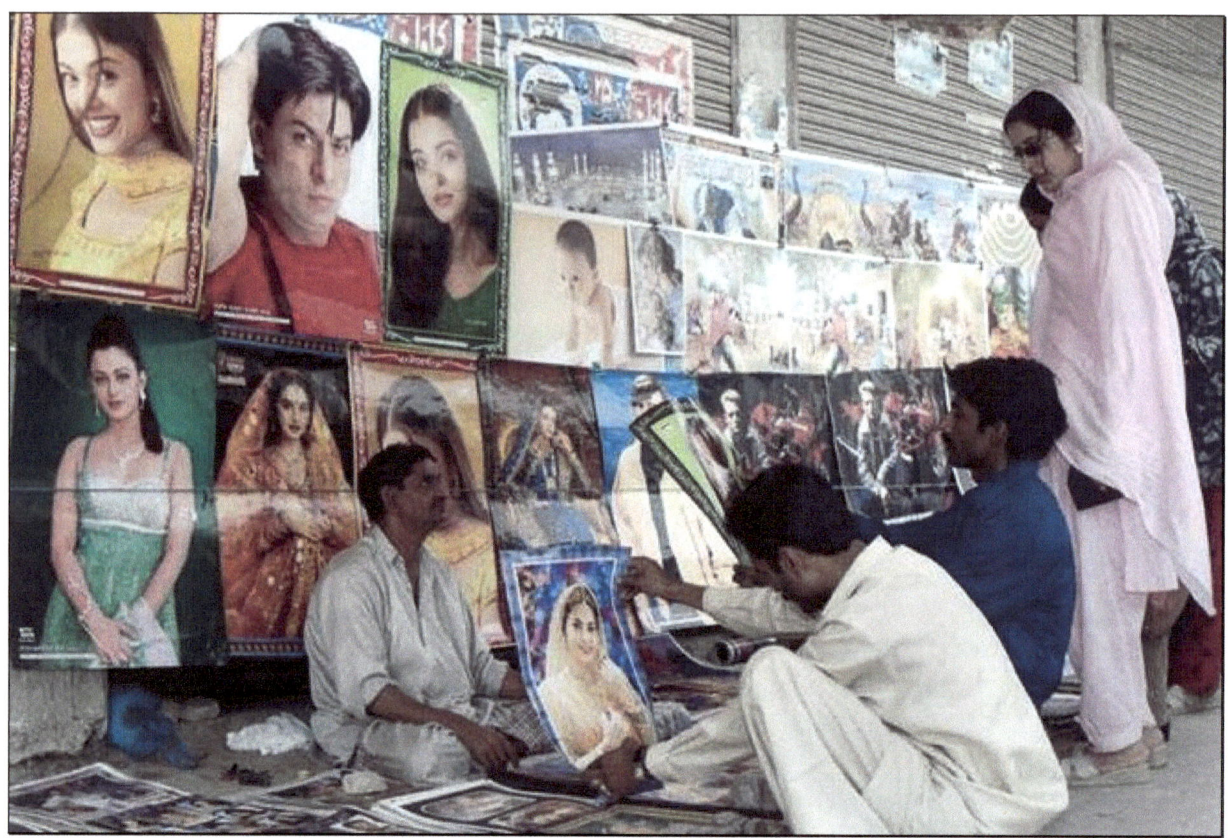

Bollywood Presence in Pakistan

Since I have been associated with Bollywood journalism since long time and because of my profession, I have been in good association with industry. I remember when Ali Zafar had started using Bollywood public relation companies to get work way back in 2004-2005. I was also provided press releases on the star by PR companies. The constant use of PRs finally got him work there when the stories on him began rolling in Indian media and across the globe.

Pooja Bhatt launched Rahat Fateh Ali Khan in her movie 'Paap' and in this same movie Pakistani pop sensation Ali Azmat too was roped into singing. Rahat sang the semi classical song 'Mann Ki Lagan' written by famous Pakistani poet Amjad Islam Amjad. The song became an instant hit making the singer the big star overnight. Later Rahat took time to grow in Hindi film industry.

It was in 2005 when Tips Industries gave me the task of seeking a very beautiful actress from Pakistan to star in its upcoming movie opposite Harbhajan Mann. The producers wanted something like Pakistani beauty queen. Well, the movie later shelved due to some their own reasons. Those days, Tips Industries was also on the lookout to launch Pakistani singers, they approached me for the task. I provided them the list of famous Pakistani singers and among them Rahat's name was also enlisted. The casting director asked me about Rahat specifically. I told him that he was the one who sang 'Mann Ki Lagan' for Pooja's movie. He said 'this is the singer he wants'. When I uttered to him about the lyricist's name, he asked me to help him contact Amjad Islam Amjad as he liked the poetry a lot. Few years after 'Mann Ki Lagan', Rahat was superstar in filmdom.

Legendary lyricist and poet Javed Akhtar once told to a Pakistani news channel's host 'they (Pakistani industry) need us not we (Bollywood) to grow'. To a larger extent, 'yes', he is right looking at Pakistani artists' constant visits to Bollywood. Every kid in Pakistan grows watching Hindi movies and their icons are not Pakistani movie stars but Bollywood stars. Bollywood's fan following is tremendously high in Pakistan and this had given the way to the screening of Indian movies there.

In a capsule, Bollywood is not limited to India only rather has surpassed the boundaries and exists everywhere in the world.

****

11

Do We Have Courage to Say 'Yes' to Item Numbers?

Do you expect a Hindi movie without an item number? It has become a trend and been strengthened over the years. Even today, you stumble upon the item songs in television shows. They are acceptable now by all types of viewers and seem okay since it aptly fulfills their job of churning out money for the producers. The popularity of the item numbers has transcended the boundaries and now the Pakistani cinema industry too follows this trend of injecting these songs into their movies.

The item number or item song is made and used in Indian cinema industries such as in Bollywood and other regional films of India. It is a musical song inserted into a movie and does not have any relevance to the plot. The mere use of these songs is to raise the popularity of the film and ultimately make money. It often features catchy, upbeat and sexually provocative dance sequence. The ultimate goal of an item number is to entertain the cinemagoers and to lend support to the marketability of the movie. Often they are featured in film trailers to boost up the popularity graph of the flick among the cinema lovers. Normally, this song is picturized on a girl and sometimes a boy too is roped in to shake the hips according to the nature of the content or demand. The girl, who dances in this number, is called an *item girl* and the same goes for the boy (as he is termed an *'item boy'*). The meaning of this number refers to highly sexualized song with racy imagery and suggestive lyrics.

These songs instantly catch the attention of the people with the sexual content they possess from lyrics to picturiztion and to the skin show of the woman who dances in. The musical beats of the item numbers too are quite bouncing, which energize the souls instantaneously. Often item songs are criticized due to the objectification of women, but are liked supremely at the same time as well.

Item songs in Hindi filmdom are not new at all rather according to history have begun to be inserted into film narrative since 1930s. Azoorie performed on many item numbers in 1930s era. Later the trend gathered momentum and kept going on. Up to 70s era, Bollywood relied quite heavily on vamps, who used to deliver item numbers as well wearing revealing clothes providing steamy and seductive atmosphere in songs.

In 50s, 60s and 70s eras, Helen came into limelight with her classy and electrifying dancing moves. The songs such as *Mera Naam Chin Chin Choo, Piya Tu Ab To Aaja, Mungda* and *Mehbooba Mehbooba* are still fresh among the masses.

Iconic actress Madhuri Dixit is considered to be the pioneer of the modern trend of item songs. In late 80s, the song *'Ek Do Teen'* from the film *'Tezaab'* made her mega star overnight. Dixit's association with legendary choreographer Saroj Khan gave numerous hits like the controversial song *'Cholie Ke Peeche Kiya Hai'* and *'Dhak Dhak'*. Media reports after Khalnayak release suggest that the people came out to watch the movie just because of *'Cholie Ke Peeche Kiya Hai'*.

Although the leading actresses of cinema industry have been the part of these numbers since long time back, but since early 2000 this trend of featuring the lead actresses into item songs has gathered much strength. This is because of the instant fame and bomb of money offered to them – then why to say 'no'? Gone are the days when the item songs were only restricted to item girls, today you witness the leading brigade of the industry shaking their hips on the beats of these songs. The term *'item girl'* has faded away now.

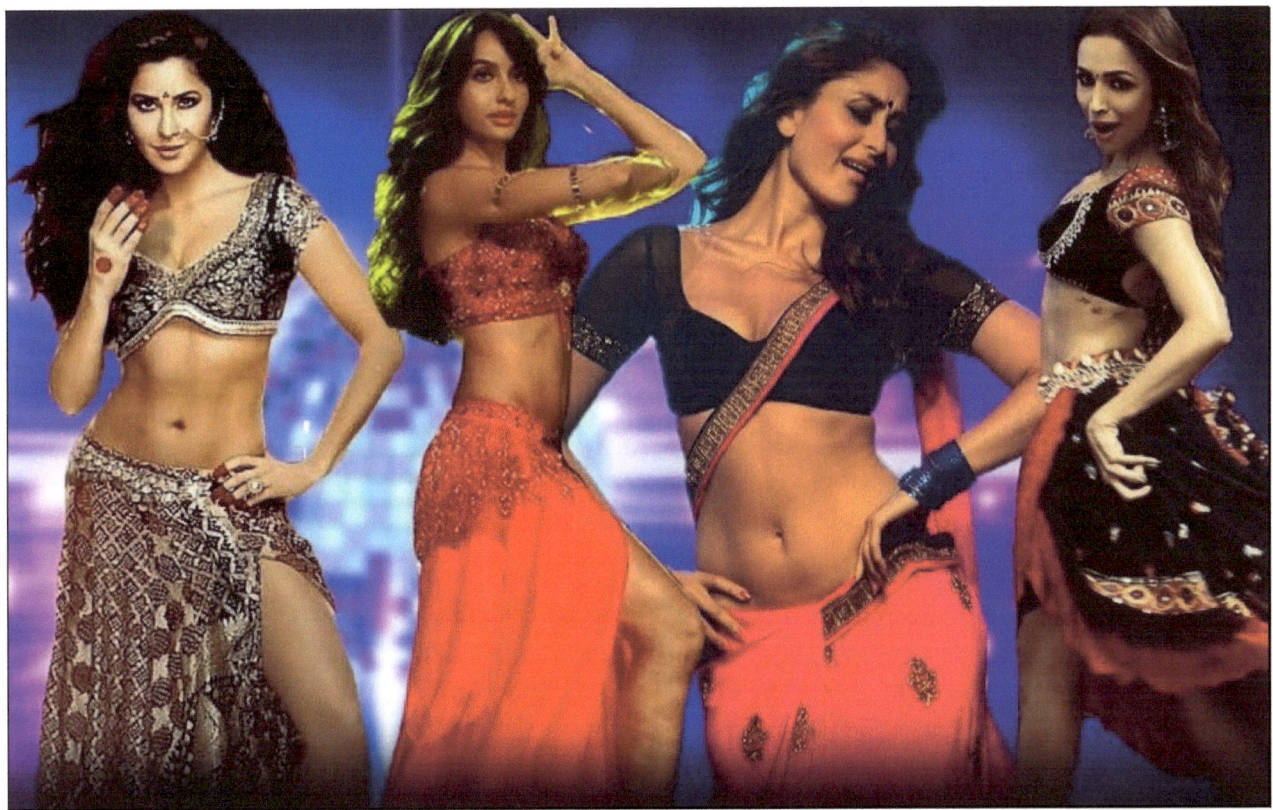

Item Number Queens of Bollywood

Year 2000 gave way to all top Bollywood actresses and many newcomers a shortcut to instant success packed with whopping amount of money in the form of item numbers. Well, it was heavily followed and still continues with oomph. You name it and almost every leading actress has it in her kitty. They find them more lucrative for their success and money and these numbers are preferred since the fact remains that the traditional roles even do not give any guarantee of stardom many a time, but item songs do instead. Rakhi Sawant and Meghna Naidu once ruled the scene with their songs and even were offered pivotal roles in movies later.

Malaika Arora once told that she did not want to act in films as she earned more than enough money by just doing an item number as opposed to major roles in movies. Aishwarya Rai's item song *'Kajra Re'* from *'Bunty Aur Babli'* was a major hit of 2005.

Abhishek Bachchan is said to be the first *'item boy'* with his dance performance in the movie *'Rakht'*. Later all top actors turned out to be the same. Shah Rukh Khan did *'Dard-e-Disco'* in *'Om Shanti Om'*. Hrithik Roshan did for the movie *'Krazzy 4'* and Ranbir Kapoor danced on an item song in *'Chillar Party'*.

In 2010, the item numbers such as *'Sheila Ki Jawani'* from *'Tees Maar Khan'* and *'Munni Badnaam Hui'* from *'Dabangg'* hit the jackpot. Both Katrina Kaif and Malaika Arora then turned out to be the best choices for these specific songs. 2012's superhit song *'Chikni Chameli'* from *'Agneepath'* took Kaif's popularity to highest level.

Deepika Padukone did the numbers such as *'Party On My Mind'* and *'Lovely'*. Priyanka Chopra went to do *'Babli Badmash'*, *'Pinky'* and *'Ram Chahe Leela'*. Sunny Leone hogged the limelight with the songs *'Baby Doll'* and *'Laila'*. Moroccon-Canadian belly dancer Nora Fatehi did *'Dilbar'* that has become the most popular music video of all time.

To perform on an item number today, every A-List actress wants to be featured in. The desire is vivid since massive fame and instant mammoth money is offered. The actresses or even the actors, whom popularity graph has dropped, are always on the look for these songs. According to reports and sources, the leading actresses are paid in crores for just one piece of item song. Reportedly the top notch brigade of Bollywood is paid 2 to 5 crores (in between) for an item number. Since the display of skin is quite high in these kinds of songs apart from the racy lyrics and hot picturization, the leading actresses of film industry make these numbers more strapping with their appearances and dancing moves. Item number is made with utter carefulness since the filmmakers are aware of its importance. It is film's marketing and promotion tool and sells the movie before its release. It drags the audiences to cinema halls. Every actress today is keen to be taken onboard in these songs and very proudly reveals the skin.

We all like to watch item number no matter if the controversies are out there – even the ones who create controversies, they too internally want to see the hip shaking of the actresses on celluloid. Then why to say *'no'*? Be brave and say *'yes'* to item songs.

****

12

Bollywood Awaits Donal Bisht – Is She Ready?

I came to know about this talented actress when I was to write a cover story on her. And to do this, I needed to talk to her. The first interaction was simply awesome, as she happened to be a great human being and her actress persona was far away, which I often find with celebrities. More than one and a half year has gone now and I always find her a very sweet, amiable, friendly and professional actress. I have written a number of stories on Bisht so far and this let me have the chance of talking to her. Although she has done numerous shows on television and today is rated high in TV fraternity, but Donal does not have any tantrums, which one witnesses a lot with high profile celebrities. If you are in the field of journalism, you even stumble upon many low profile stars who keep flaunting off tantrums. But this actress is devoid of any kind of misbehavior especially with the journalists.

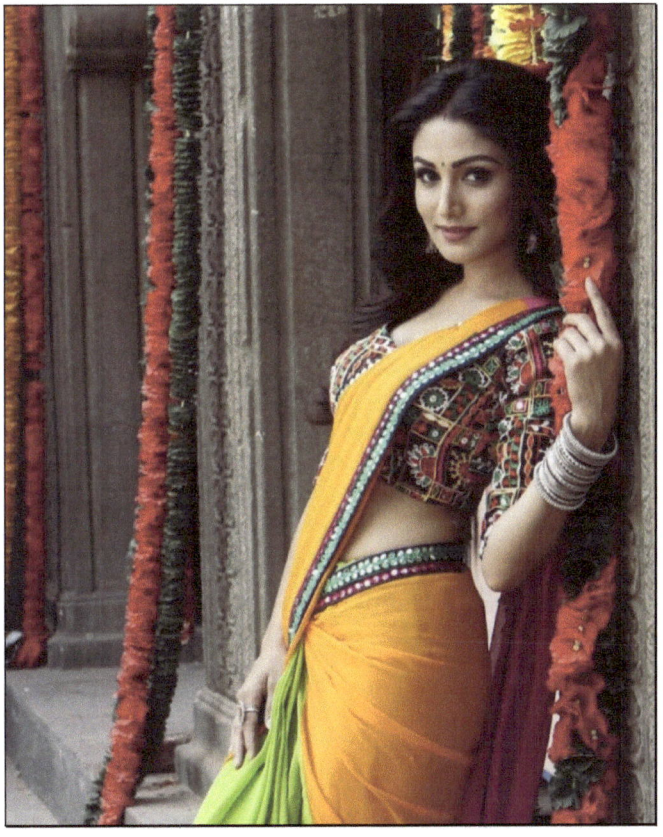

Donal Bisht

In my long journalistic career, I have interviewed so many stars and have been interacting with majority of the Bollywood and television industries, I found only few who happened to be amiable and sweet human beings and Donal Bisht is one of them.

She shot to fame with Colors TV show *'Roop - Mard Ka Naya Swaroop'* and because of this Bisht is being noticed by the critics for her exceptional acting skills and screen persona. She has now landed into demands not only from small industry but also from Bollywood and web series. Donal is quite choosy after her soft image she has registered with the masses with her character of Ishika Patel. Since entire entertainment industry of India has turned to the big demand of web series, she too is being offered the leading roles for this genre of filmmaking. I talked to her about the same to learn as to what was stopping her to say *'yes'* to these offers? The answer I got showed how sensitive and careful she was for her career? Bisht revealed that web series was all about nudity, and she did not want to be a part of it, as her soft image which had developed among her fans would be shattered if she slipped into the flow of web series.

Donal Bisht is getting offers from Bollywood as well, but will accept the one where she finds a better role to display. Her final destination is of course Hindi cinema industry, but to conquer there she awaits the right script. She is a newcomer in the industry and has few shows to her credit so far, but the acting prowess she possesses has taken her to heights which the A-Listers enjoy. Recently Donal was ranked 18th in Times of India's Top 20 Most Desirable Women on TV. She has a long way to go and her gradual steps towards big success will surely make ways for her.

****

13

From Modeling to Acting and Now Film Censor Board – Maushmi Udeshi

Well-known model turned actress Maushmi Udeshi got instant fame when she did a television commercial for Nescafe and later a music video *'Noorie'* with Bali Sagoo. She started off her career way back in 2002 and since then she has been endowing her fans and the masses with numerous jobs of music videos, ads, fashion shoots and acting. I know Maushmi since the beginning of her career and this association is quite old. She is nice, sweet and sensitive person. I know Udeshi deeply and am quite aware of her dreams to make big in life. And, *'yes'*, she has achieved a lot with her sheer hard work, passion and struggle. Mausam (her nickname, and I always call her with the same) is equipped with multi talents and is well-aware of the skills she possesses. She knows the art of presenting those skills into work and this is her mantra for success.

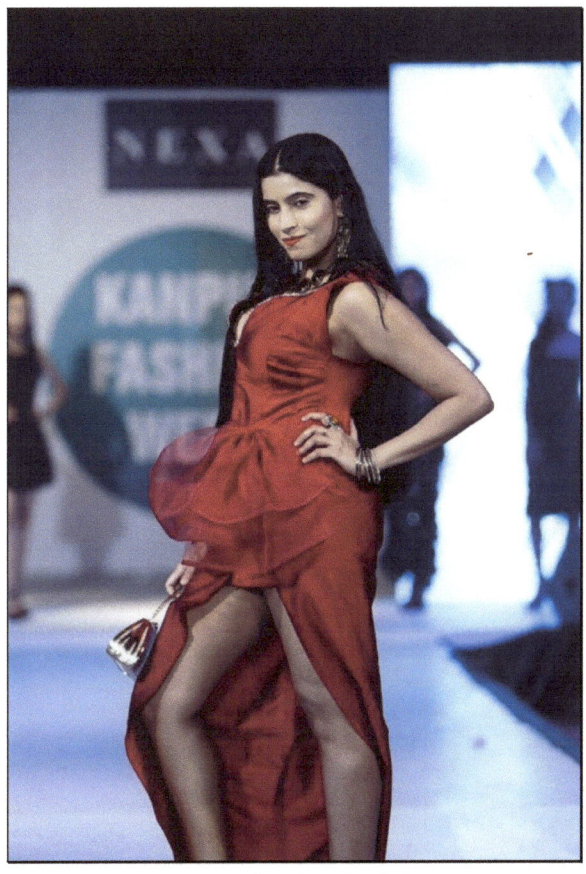

Maushmi Udeshi

Today, Maushmi is a member of the advisory board of the film censor of India apart from being actress and a fashion model. The utter credit for her success goes to her struggle and passion she has done with conviction.

Mausam has been the face for many renowned Indian magazines' cover pages. Her photoshoots always garnish fame and turn out to be central focus of the people. She has worked with all leading photographers of the industry. The sensuous persona, Udeshi s laced with, works big time whenever she comes in front of the camera. She is a confident actress and the facial expressions and dialogue delivery she displays make her the best of the lot.

Post the giant success of Munna Bhai MBBS, one night while I was talking to her, she revealed that she was offered the hit song *'Dekh Le'*, but due to some reasons could not be the part of the track. Eventually item girl Mumait Khan was later roped in to do it. Item number *'Aafareen'* in Priyadarshan's comic caper *'Bhagam Bhaag'* added big values to Maushmi's career.

She has been the show stopper at a number of fashion shows in India and has walked the ramps in many others as well. Mausam has done numerous music videos in south also. She was conferred with the *'Rashtra Shakti Gaurav Award'* on January 23, 2011 for being the best model in ad films and music videos. She is a known face in web movies as well. She is currently doing a movie with Rajpal Yadav. Maushmi Udeshi is undoubtedly the best model and actress to be raved big about.

****